EL SEGUNDO PUBLIC LIBRARY

3 5156 00449 7367

D0771060

J 582 STON
Ston
Fruit

DISCARDED

DUE

El Segundo Public Library

J 582 STON
Stone, Lynn M.
Fruit   c.1

Fruit

Lynn Stone

Rourke
Publishing LLC
Vero Beach, Florida 32964

APR 2 2 2008

© 2008 Rourke Publishing LLC

All rights reserved. No part of this book may be reproduced or utilized in any form or by any means, electronic or mechanical including photocopying, recording, or by any information storage and retrieval system without permission in writing from the publisher.

www.rourkepublishing.com

PHOTO CREDITS: All photos © Lynn M. Stone except, pg.4 © Ellen Hart; pg.6a © Leksandr Starposeltsev; pg.6b © Michael Hill; pg.6c © Krzysiek z Poczty; pg.9 © Ivan Vodnev; pg.10 © Christopher Ewing; pg.12a © Engin Communication; pg.12b,12c © Diane Rutt; pg.12d © Edd Westmacott; pg.12e © Achim Prill; pg.14a, 14b © Suzannah Skelton; pg.14c © Norman Chan; pg.16 © Laura Thomas; pg.20 © Jerzy Czarkowski; pg.21 © Dusan Zidar.

Editor: Robert Stengard-Olliges

Cover design by: Nicola Stratford, bdpublishing.com

Library of Congress Cataloging-in-Publication Data

Stone, Lynn M.
 Fruit / Lynn Stone.
    p. cm. -- (Plant parts)
 ISBN 978-1-60044-552-1 (Hardcover)
 ISBN 978-1-60044-692-4 (Softcover)
 1. Fruit--Juvenile literature. I. Title.
 QK660.S86 2008
 581.4'64--dc22

                        2007015156

Printed in the USA

CG/CG

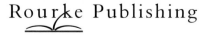

www.rourkepublishing.com – rourke@rourkepublishing.com
Post Office Box 3328, Vero Beach, FL 32964

Table of Contents

More Than Food

You may know fruits just as sweet and juicy treats. But fruits are more than just food for people and wild animals.

Plants make fruits to help protect their seeds. Seeds are important because they make new plants.

Fruit

Seeds

The seeds grow in a part of the plant's flower called the ovary. The ovary grows larger and becomes fruit. The seeds stay inside the growing ovary.

Ovary

In time, the ovary and seeds finish growing. The fruit is now **ripe**. A fruit is a plant's ripe ovary with seeds inside.

Many well known fruits are soft and fleshy. **Berries** and cherries are fleshy fruits. So are grapes and bananas.

12

Fruit or Vegetable?

Some plants that we call vegetables are actually fruits. Tomatoes are a good example. **Peppers** and cucumbers are fruits, too. If it has seeds, then it is a fruit.

Are pumpkins fruits? Have you ever cut open a pumpkin for Halloween? If you have, you know that pumpkins are full of seeds. Pumpkins are fruits.

Even More Fruit

Many fruits are not soft at all. The milkweed plant makes a crispy cover around its seeds. This type of dry fruit is often called a **pod**.

There are many types of fruit. Lemons, oranges, pineapples, bananas, apples and **chestnuts** are all fruit.

Chestnut

Nut

Fruit

Glossary

berries (BER ees) — a small fleshy fruit with many seeds

chestnut (CHESS nuht) — a large nut that grows in a prickly fruit

ovary (OH vur ee) — the part of the plant that forms seeds

peppers (PEP uhrs) — large bell-shaped fruits

pod (POD) — a seed-case of a flowering plant

ripe (RIPE) — at its completed stage of growth

Index

Further Reading

Bodach, Vijaya and Saunders-Smith, Gail. *Fruit*. Capstone, 2006.

Farndon, John. *Fruits*. Thomson Gale, 2006.

Websites to Visit

www.kathimitchell.com/plants.html

www.picadome.fcps.net/lab/currl/plants/default.htm

About the Author

Lynn M. Stone is the author of more than 400 children's books. He is a talented natural history photographer as well. Lynn, a former teacher, travels worldwide to photograph wildlife in its natural habitat.